The Now Exspirientuality

∽

The Way of Unity

Greg Allen Morgoglione
with Alice, the Canine Messiah

Conversations with Dog - Book 1

Copyright © 2009 Greg Allen Morgoglione
All rights reserved.

ISBN: 1-4392-5927-5
ISBN-13: 9781439259276
Library of Congress Control Number: 2009910619

This book and the CD *It's Time That Time Was Overthrown* are dedicated to...

...Community Venue audiences and the Opportunity they present for our society. It is our intent that this book raises awareness of the Opportunity. It is our hope that more musicians will Look Again, begin to live their lyrics, and share their Absoulute Gifts of time and talent with you. For their sake...

...staff at Community Venues that have supported SongSharing by treating performances as performances. We appreciate the respect you show for the Fellow Beings in your care, and your recognition of the Opportunity they afford us. We also love it when you dance and sing and clap along.

...inspired musicians.

...aspiring musicians. May you find that it's Inspiration.

Contents

Preface	vii
An Illusion of Time	xvi
In the Beginning	xxi
Nothing to Add	xxii
Acknowledgements	xvii
The Messiah Is In	xxiii
Introduction	xxxv

Part 1

An Alice poem (Opportunity for Unity)	1
A Now Exspirientuality Story	3
Perspective on a Now Point of View	5
The One Exercise: Preface	13
An Absolute Attitude	15
The One Exercise: *Meditation on the Streets of Your Life*	17
The Act of Being	21
An Alice poem (The Need to No)	23
Thoughtless Awareness, the Fruit, and the LifeDreamBoat	25
An Alice poem (At Dawn)	29
It's Time That Time Was Overthrown: CD Lyrics	

Part 2

Creation and ReCreation	49
Showmen/Shaman	53
The Now Exspirientuality and KCRC	55
Samzan's Enlightenment	59
The Opportunity of Opportunity	61

Preface

Sometimes it seems as though This Here Now is the problem for Utopia-singing, aspiring folk stars. The logic is something like, "Clearly This Here Now is a problem, because Look at Them, over There. This world is a mess, for They should not have to (or choose to) Be like That. No one should have to (or choose to) Be like That. Let me write a song to lament This Here Now and another to sing about how great things will be in my Dream of That There Then, where and when no one has to (or chooses to) Be like Them."

I've been asking musicians in my town to go beyond traditional acoustic venues and share their music in Community Venues for the better part of the last decade. Outside of a small group of folks that have proven to be persistently supportive, the overwhelming response has been some variant of "I don't have time." Not an hour in over a decade... This response was the inspiration for *It's Time That Time Was Overthrown*. I'm convinced they believe Time hangs on a wall and orders them and their Life about.

And I am sometimes certain that a big part of the reason musicians will not come is that they believe that Community Venue audiences fall in the "Special Needs – Music" category and are thus somehow less than the best; they are somehow of diminished music business value.

It's as though musicians imagine there is an *Album for Amputees,* or a *Songs for Seniors* CD that they must cover; as though they must follow and learn songs from the *Developmentally Disabled Top 40* in order for a Community Venue audience to "get it." It's as though "Music is a universal language, except that They would not get my music." It's as though the idea of transcendence does not apply to the perceived Special Musical Needs of a Community Venue audience.

Sometimes I even imagine that Utopian-singing musicians Dream of a world where Equality means that no one has to "Be Like" the people in Community Venue audiences. In their Dream world there will be no "old people," or "disabled people," or "sick" or "suffering" people, or whatever they imagine these Fellow Beings to be Being. When the world is free of "people like Them," these musicians might truly be able to sing freely and celebrate the Joy of Being freely and openly, without thought of monetary worth; without fear that someone won't "get it" – or buy it....

In the meantime though, let's keep the Other-based-blues alive. It's a tough world, because, well, "Look at Them. That sucks, to Be like Them. My vision is of a world free of Being like Them." And off they go to sing *about* Them, or do a benefit *for* Them; but never anything *with* Them. It's no fun to hang out with people you don't want to Be like, I suppose.

I notice, too, that it seems the further away They are in space and time, the more appeal there is to doing something *about* or *for* Them. Many musicians that did not have an hour in a decade for a Community Venue audience had plenty of time to help stage shows that benefited Katrina victims half a country away, or tsunami victims, or Darfur refugees half a world away.

But disabled Fellow Beings, right Here? Seniors, in my own Community? My neighbors? Grab a cup of coffee and my guitar and go play for an hour and make some new friends and fans? Outside of my demographic? Huh?

Be the Change I sing of seeing in my world? Huh?

> *There's the progress: We have found*
> *A way to sing around the problem*
> *Building towered foresight isn't anything at all.*
>
> …from R.E.M.'s *Fall On Me*[1]

Sometimes it seems as though This Here Now is a problem for Utopia-talking spiritual seekers. The logic is something like, "Clearly This Here Now is a problem, because Look at Them, over There. This world is a mess, for They should not have to (or choose to) Be like That. No one should have to (or choose to) Be like That. Let me find another book that laments This Here Now, and yet another with steps to a Dream of That There Then, where and when no one has to Be like Them."

I've been asking spiritual seekers both personally and in on-line forums to engage the practice of visits to Community Venues for the last several years—not because they happen to also be musicians, but precisely because they are spiritual seekers, and precisely because every one of us has human artistic Gifts to share. Many long to reclaim these and seek an appropriate Life venue within which to share them.

Most of them, like musicians, have proven to "not have time." I'm convinced they also believe Time hangs on a wall and orders them and their Lives about. There is an especially odd quality when the encounter is in a forum about living in the present moment, the wildly popular "now."

And I am sometimes certain that a big part of the reason spiritual seekers will not engage Compassionate Behavior – like sharing some time, love, and humanity with people in Community Venues – is that they simply enjoy seeking. Mostly they seem to enjoy the martyr-like misery and loneliness of seeking, for they ignore countless Opportunities to engage in spiritual behavior. To firm up their need for steps away from

Here, many spiritual seekers seem to surround themselves with a close inner circle of folks that are particularly spiritually challenging. Meanwhile they steadfastly ignore the Opportunity of countless folks available to them who would be very grateful for a spiritual sort of encounter, a few minutes of simple Humanity for no reason other than a few minutes of simple Humanity.

The Opportunity of neighbors on the bus and the subway, folks on the street, and local homeless folks and hungry folks is ignored; the Opportunity of community members in senior homes, nursing homes and facilities for our disabled neighbors; the Opportunity of neighbors that rarely, or never, get a visitor. Countless folks presenting the Opportunity to Express and Experience Life *Just As I Am* are perpetually ignored. "My time is not for that…"

It's as though spiritual seekers imagine some folks to be "Special Needs – Spiritual", or "Special Needs – Humanity". It's as though *Just As I Am* is different with some people, different in Community Venues.

And sometimes I even imagine that Utopian-talking spiritual seekers Dream of a world where Equality means that no one has to "Be Like" the people in Community Venue audiences. In their Dream world, there will be no "old people," or "disabled people," or "sick" or "suffering" people, or whatever they imagine these Fellow Beings to be Being. When the world is free of "people like Them," these seekers will finally feel at home, truly able to celebrate the Joy of Being freely and openly, without thought of spiritual payoff, without fear that something spiritual might not happen.

In the meantime though, it's a tough world, because, well, "Look at Them. That must suck, to Be like Them." And off they go to be sad *about* Them, or meditate or pray *for* Them, or send money to an organization that helps Them; but rarely if ever do they take twenty-five minutes to simply do the human thing – the spiritual human thing – *with* Them.

I notice, too, that it seems the further away They are in space and time, the more appeal there is to doing something *about* or *for* Them. Most seekers that do not have the time to visit someone in a Community Venue have plenty of time to chatter away online about their concerns for the folks the musicians are performing about at their benefit shows.

But disabled Fellow Beings, right Here? Seniors, in my own Community? My neighbors? Grab a cup of coffee and my desire to Express and Experience Humanity? Now? Right Now, you mean? While I am alive?

What? Be the Change I expect Others to be in my world? First? Huh?

A Dream

We can get along. Now.
We can share. Now.
There is enough. Now.
This Here Now Is It.

And there are of course the non-spiritual and anti-spiritual seekers, and sometimes it seems as though This Here Now is their problem as well. For many of them, the big problem with This Here Now is precisely the spiritual seekers. Together they're arguing and Living for a different That There Then. It's a sad and funny sort of interdependence.

Sometimes I'm convinced that the non- and anti-spiritual seekers are the funny ones. They too have stories of how it all began with One Thing and will return to One Thing, and their sciences that tell them This Here Now is, beyond doubt, One Thing. They even have sciences wherein they are witnessing the basic premise of The One Exercise; wherein they now see that One Thing can simultaneously be in more than One Place at the same time. They speak of The Central Singularity, but they can't allow for a minute that the idea behind the word God might be analogous to the idea behind the term Central Singularity. This is mostly because they do not envision their Central Singularity as a cosmic Caucasian male with a beard, a throne, and a justice stick.

What they're missing is their steadfast clinging to childish ideas that God is any such thing, and that God is "out There" somewhere. Nothing is separate in Unity. The Central Singularity is ever present. Look Again.

༄

And sometimes it seems as though This Here Now is the big problem for our society. To hear the news media report it and our leaders tell it, the big problem is This Here Now.

"Clearly This Here Now is a problem, because Those Others over There continue to Be like That. Look at Them, over There. And That. They should not Be Like That, or Do That, or Say That, or Be Subjected to That. We must take these steps to get us away from This Here Now."

And sometimes I imagine that society has the vague idea that This Here Now will remain inadequate until the people in Darfur have laptops, X-boxes, and a car or two, along with everyone else on the planet. A "green" car, of course. The Good Thing will remain distant until folks that live or vacation on the coast face no possibility of hurricanes or tsunamis. It'd be great to rid the world of those little squalls that ruin our afternoon cookouts as well.

And sometimes I am certain that society thus agrees with the musicians and the spiritual seekers that The Good Thing will be recognized in part by the absence of many types of perceived Others. To hear the news media report it and our leaders tell it, it's a long list of Others creating Life's problems, challenges, and obligations for us; Poor Others and Bad Others and Evil Others and Other Others too...

And sometimes it seems as though the greatest appeal for society as well is to champion the cause of the most distant Poor Other, at the expense of the nearest Fellow Being. Every day it seems that most of society walks past Opportunity on the streets of its hometown....

What? Be the Change I expect Others to be in my world? Me? First? Actually make a difference Here, Now? Face to face? Huh?

Every day it seems we miss the simple Opportunity to Think Global, Act Local. It's the Opportunity to heal our world in This moment.

∽

Sometimes it seems like all that....

∽

*An Illusion of Time is that Time will Get You to
Where You Have Long Dreamed of Being*

∽

*The Truth about Time Is That
Time Is Where You Have Long Dreamed of Being*

∽

*Now. What Are You Being?
What Are You Choosing to Be, Here Now, In Time?*

∽

What's Your Dream?

from What Would Dog Do?:
The Canine Messiah's Handbook

∽

Acknowledgements

I must express deepest and most profound gratitude to…

…my parents and my sister. Thanks beyond thanks for Being you. Thanks for everything I could list, and some things I have likely forgotten.

…my grandfather Louis Carroll Carey; for the incredible sense of humor and respectful irreverence for just about everything. Thanks for always being here for me, especially after you moved on.

…Mrs. Laura Robb.

…my girlfriend, Lynn, and our beloved pack: PinkE, Yugen, Alice, Arlo, and Sevon.

…Fuzzy, Pickles, Angus, Patch, Quincy, Sam, and all of the wonderful dogs that have shared their Time with me. Rest in Peace; play like hell, baby…

…Oodles, Casper, and Marvin; for providing the feline balance.

…Nedra, Clara, and aunt Alice.

…the local musicians that have supported SongSharing™, especially Granville Braxton, Thomas Gunn, Tom Proutt and Emily Gary, Julie Caran, Abbey Linfert and Chris Amsler, and Jeff Romano.

...Iris, activities director at Heritage Hall who had the foresight and talent to establish a successful, staff-supported, evening concert series at a nursing home in 1995.

...to the musicians that donated to *CDs for the Troops* in 2003. The overwhelming support for this effort greatly inspired the '04 formalization of SongSharing as a non-profit.

Dana and Susan Robinson, Paul Rishell and Annie Raines, Andrew McKnight, Dean Fields, Dave Crossland, Zoe Mulford, David Wilcox, and Slaid Cleaves; for living your lyrics and for your stunningly down-to-earth Community Venue performances.

Hunter Johnson and Brooke.

The fine folks that are the R.E.M./Athens organization; for every bit of support you have ever given SongSharing. Your *"of course* we'll participate" approach to participation in the 2003 *CDs for the Troops* effort lent great momentum to SongSharing's establishment as a non-profit, and the precedent you set continues to open doors for us. Especially thanks to David Bell and Kevin O'Neil, for your patience and desire to understand and support the SongSharing mission – even though we are 500 miles from Athens...

Bill Berry, Peter Buck, Mike Mills, and Michael Stipe; for the R.E.M. / Athens organization. Role model, baby. Also for the stunning music catalog, and the lyrics. Oh my, the lyrics...

Mr. Billy Joel, for autographing the Baldwin piano; and your fine staff, for helping make it happen. Gracious, countless times over....

Joe Imbriaco and his staff at John Paul Jones Arena in Charlottesville, Virginia, for your invaluable help in arranging the aforementioned Billy Joel autograph.

Ms. Dolly Parton, for autographing *the washboard Jolene;* and to Ms. Theresa Hughes of Velvet Apple Publishing for helping make it happen.

Rodney and Matt at Rodney Mills Masterhouse.

Ms. Kenne Driver, for all those Sunday mornings of fresh fruit and philosophy. You showed me the value of giving oneself away.

Ms. Ellen Luksch, for too much to list here, but particularly for reminding me of the mirror.

Ms. Susan Wright, for your valuable time and input.

the late Alan Watts, and the folks who keep his legacy alive.

the late Joseph Campbell, and the folks who keep his legacy alive.

Eckhart Tolle, for the stunning simplicity, and mostly for the sincerity without all the seriousness.

Neale Donald Walsch, wherever he may find HimSelf; and mirrors.

Justin Hyman, for countless hours of wonderfully fun and insightful conversations.

MadCo Agility students and their dogs, and the canine agility world in general. You have shown me things…

Sam, Jim, Tim, Melissa and the Army Of Darkness Motorcycle Endurance Racing Team.

∞

IN THE BEGINNING THERE IS GOD.
Reflecting upon AllSelf and All That Is, God says
"I Am That. That I Am."

And That is all good, and That I Am is a good beginning.

AND THE REFLECTION OF GOD IS GOD
and perceiving ItSelf as The Original Reflection
(and imagining a mirror)
Dog says, "I Am That's Am. That Sam I Am."

And That is good, and That Sam is a good dog.

∞

from Digging the Whole:
The Canine Book of Play

∽

*A Messiah's primary function among Humans
Is to remind them, over and over,
That they are, Here Now,
Perfect Expressions of the Universe.*

∽

There is Nothing to Add

from What Would Dog Do?:
The Canine Messiah's Handbook

∽

The Messiah Is In

In April of 2005 I found myself in Buckingham County, Virginia, way out in the midst of nowhere, a dozen dusty miles deep into gravel roads and young pine forests. I was looking for a particular home for which a friend had asked me to provide a price opinion. The directions had failed to mention the poor signage along the way, and although I was fairly confident that this was the correct road, there was still a certain attendant sense of being lost, even alone. If this was not the correct road, I wouldn't be stopping to ask directions. I had not seen a house for the last eight miles, easily – it wasn't long after I left the highway.

As I came around a bend – what would prove to be the next to last bend in the road prior to the fork in the road where the house in question was situated – I saw a small table ahead, on the side of the road, in the ample shade of roadside trees. Like a child's lemonade stand perhaps – I could see a chair, a table with some stuff on it, and a sign. No people, though, and as I got closer I saw a small dog lying next to the table. She moved into a sitting position as I pulled closer and slowed. I got out and walked around the car. What she had for a tail was wagging as she stood to greet me.

"Hey, little girl!" I smiled and bent down to pet her. "What are you doing out here all alone?"

She appeared very healthy, and happy, and glad to see me I thought. She had a soft slip-collar around her neck, attached to a leash that was attached to a leg of the table. There was a dish of water nearby, and she seemed comfortable enough – the sun would be setting soon. Red miniature pinscher, ears naturally floppy, tail cropped by an amateur. She was a bit big for the breed, beautiful color, deep bright eyes. She gazed at me rather intently.

I glanced at the easel that stood next to the table, and chuckled at the sign that said "The Messiah Is In" – I recall thinking back to the *Peanuts* comic strips, and the little stand Lucy had for advice. I wondered where The Messiah was, and I wondered why on earth any sort of stand would be set up in the middle of nowhere squared.

"Where's The Messiah, you cute little girl?" I asked her. "Yeah right," I thought aloud, and I smiled in her direction.

As the light breeze began to pick up, I surveyed the card table. It was new, very clean. On it was a small pad of paper, a pen, a cheap plastic mechanical pencil, and a rock. Smooth and rounded like a stone you'd find near a lake or river, the rock seemed out of place here. It had not been found nearby, by someone in a hurry to leave that needed a paperweight. The breeze fluttered up the edges of a handwritten note underneath – a page torn from the pad, a pleasant lazy printing in fine pencil, likely the mechanical one.

> *Thanks for stopping by...*
> *I had to leave in a hurry –*
> *please take care of the dog for Now –*
> *she's One of a kind – an Absoulute Lover!*
> *Thanks again.*
> *Best of Now, Always...*

I looked at the dog. I looked at the note. I looked around. I remember distinctly, at that moment, just having that feeling, that "oh no!" sort of knowing, that Lynn and I were about to add a dog to the pack. She was adorable. I kept my cool though, and tried to think of rational reasons this dog would be here, and this note. I couldn't come up with any.

I loosened the leash from the table leg, and took her for a walk. She peed twice, and we headed for the Honda. I slipped the collar-leash over her head, lifted her up, opened the passenger door, and tossed the leash in the floor. "Come on, young lady, you're coming with me. At least for a few minutes." I set her on the seat, opened the window halfway – I had left the car running – so she couldn't lock me out by stepping on a power lock switch, and walked back to the table to leave a note.

I found your dog and your note, and so I took her with me. Was uncertain who your note was intended for, but I could not leave her here alone. I am from the Charlottesville area, and you can reach me at 555-2542. I will also contact the SPCA in Buckingham.

Peace, Greg

I got in the car and we drove ahead to find the house, in the fork, just around the next bend.

༄

I made notes. I took a few photos in the fading daylight. The sun was fairly deep now behind the pines as we left the house and began to make our way back along the miles of dusty gravel roads. I slowed as we came again to the Messiah's stand – hoping for some sign of life – but I quickly began to accelerate as a "yeah, right!" knowing flashed, a bit more pronounced than the "oh no!" knowing. Less than twelve minutes had passed since I had put this cute little dog in my car. No one had come and gone that quickly, and besides, the table was still here.

"No one's here, little girl," I said aloud. "Look's like you're coming home with me, for now. You get to meet Arlo and Yugen and Quincy and Sam and PinkE and Patch. I'll have to figure out how to introduce you."

I rolled up the windows to keep the dust out, and picked up speed.

༄

We were nearing the highway, and I began to slow for the stop sign. I glanced at her, lying on the seat quietly, and then...

Alice.

Did I hear something?

Alice.

...and before thought had time to materialize I heard myself say aloud, "Is your name Alice?" I laughed, surprised at myself, as I looked at her. She had moved to the passenger floor, and was staring me straight in the eye, her little ears flopped over towards me, head cocked just a touch to one side, lips stretching slightly into a gentle canine smile.

Yes, Alice.

"That was eerie," I thought, and noticed the little hairs on the back of my ears standing up in agreement.

I listened for more. Nothing.

∽

And in the silence, I remembered Heritage Hall, Clara, and aunt Alice. Clara and aunt Alice were my first Community Venue[1] audience; I began weekly musical visits to their room at

---

1   Community Venues are non-traditional performance venues that have been a part of my monthly singer-songwriter performance schedule since 1995. Community Venues include senior homes and nursing homes, as well as the growing number of senior communities that continue to be built for our aging population. They also include facilities for our disabled neighbors such as the Kluge Children's Rehabilitation Center, Region 10's *Horizon Clubhouse*, and Arc of the Piedmont in our area. This population segment is also on the rise, as is that of military disabled.

Community Venues might also include incarcerated populations, hospitals, schools, etc. The Opportunity is huge and so far virtually unexplored as these audiences are generally regarded as being of lesser value by the business of music (and the arts) and aspiring business of music musicians.

Community Venues hold tremendous potential for everyone. It's not just a musician thing.

Heritage Hall in 1995. My friend Nedra, Clara's daughter and Alice's niece, had talked me into it...

You see, I had this idea that "their generation" wouldn't really like my original songs, and the covers I did were more contemporary artists; artists I was sure they had not heard of. I guess I had this idea that if these ladies came into a coffee shop where I was playing that they would not enjoy the music.

I think aunt Alice must have told everyone in the place, for soon her friends began to come listen. In a couple months crowds began to spill into the hallway, and then I was asked to stop in this room and that room to share a song with those who were less mobile, on my way back to work. And very soon those weekly lunchtime visits became evening concerts in the dining hall, due in large part to the encouragement of aunt Alice.

The big thing Alice encouraged was the music – *my* music. She loved it all. She sang and she danced and she laughed and clapped and carried on like a kid. She had favorites – from *my* repertoire – and she requested them, even when her memory began to slip and she could not recall the titles... Alice showed me beyond doubt that music transcends all perceived distance between humans, and that every audience is the best. Alice encouraged me immediately into a life of Making Music More Accessible™[2] and Audience Inclusion[3] through SongSharing; and ultimately into a life as a musician/magician.

---

2   *Making Music More Accessible* is a trademark of SongSharing, LLC, and the short version of SongSharing's mission. SongSharing is a non-profit organization I founded to further explore the Opportunity of Community Venues and the practice of Audience Inclusion.

3   Audience Inclusion is the simple practice of including Community Venues in one's regular performance schedule. This Opportunity actually exists for most of the arts, it seems to us. It exists for young people as well, as they explore their artistic tendencies. Community Venues are also

I warmed and smiled at the memory of my dear departed friends...

"Yes. Of course. Alice. Hello, Alice. I am Greg." I was glad we were alone. I've always talked to dogs, but honestly not when one of them started the conversation. It was a bit awkward, at the time.

It was not awkward for Alice apparently. What she has for a tail wagged and she jumped back onto the passenger seat, turned a few circles, and lay down. She didn't answer, and those hairs began to relax a bit. I accelerated, nervously I suppose, and reached over to pet her. As my hands found their way to her head and I began to scratch her ears, I wondered when I would find a cell phone signal so I could call Lynn and have her get the pack ready for an introduction. There's a process you know.

༺࿓༻

It's been well over three years since I realized Alice was indeed the Messiah referred to on that sign. I often wonder exactly what happened that day. I wonder if I dreamed it, or drove into a time warp, or some kind of dimensional shift.

༺࿓༻

---

great places for adults to reconnect with some of their hobbies and passions in a wonderful setting – scrap-booking; watercolors; something as simple as reading a favorite book aloud; something as easy as listening, peacefully listening...

Not long after she arrived, I started having a recurring dream about the evening Alice found me. I dreamed that the pine forests I was driving through were actually just a thin veil of trees hiding a huge body of water – like some sort of sixth Great Lake hidden in Virginia. I dreamed of a submarine surfacing in the water in the woods in the fork, behind that house, and Alice came from that submarine. She wasn't alone, and she knew I would be along soon. Strangely, the submarine headed for the sky when it departed. Its belly lights were far too bright, and they would wake me from my sleep – and there would be Alice, lying on the bed looking at me in the soft morning light…

Time O.T.

Tell me 'bout 3. Do you ever see 3?
Just 3? Not 3 of a kind.
Tell me 'bout me, do you ever see me?
Just me? Not me defined.
I would sleep thru the night and I'd crash in
the light though I'd heard about Time Overthrown
How I could be stuck There now, stuck free There now.
What time was it? They said, "Then-Now."

Tell me 'bout 2. Do you ever meet 2?
Just 2? Not 2 of a kind.
Tell me 'bout you, do you ever know you?
Just you? Not you in your mind.
I would sleep thru the night and I'd crash in the
light 'til I dreamed about Time Overthrown
How I could be stuck There now, stuck free There now.
What time was it? I knew: "Then-Now!"

Tell me 'bout One. Do you ever be One?
Just One? Not One of a kind.
Tell me 'bout Love, do you ever live Love?
Just Love? With no other side.

Now I light up the night and I
light up the light.
I set my watch by Time Overthrown

I am not stuck There now, stuck free There now.
I'm In Time. I Am Then-Now.

I should get a watch tattoo,
close to the truth, where the
hands only point to Now.

The concepts are cool but they're short of the
truth and the truth about Then is Now.
I only can be Then-Now I will be all I will be Then-Now.

Introduction

For the past four years Alice and I have mostly focused on songwriting. In 2006 we released the CD *tales of the uneasy writer*, and in March of 2008 we released the CD *It's Time That Time Was Overthrown*.

As the *Time Overthrown* CD was coming together, we had begun to entertain the idea of creating a book to accompany it. We had included lyrics to only three of the songs in the liner notes, and only a few snippets of Alice's wisdom, and many requests came in for lyrics to more songs and more from Alice. Lots and lots of requests for more from Alice.

So we figured Now is a good Time for a book that presents *The Now Exspirientuality*, a philosophy of Unity that Alice offers up for human consideration. *Exspirientuality* is an Alice word, a combination of our words Experiential and Spirituality. Alice has quite a bit of new language for humanity to consider in our quest to experience Unity.

Most human spiritual traditions are understood to be rooted in the idea that we will – or may – enter the Experiential realm of Spirituality later. In other words we will "have" or "live" The Spiritual Experience – later. Of course, the Spiritual Experience is a vague sort of thing, and there seems to be a sense that we can at least partially "have it" while we are alive. But the general sense seems to be that it's very much later, like after we are dead and buried. Hopefully.

Alice has come to remind us that This Here Now *is* the Spiritual Experience.

Not long ago I was reading the works of a self-proclaimed spiritual messenger – complete with a circle of disciples - who has also proclaimed a need for some new form of spirituality. Of course we're encouraged to send money to support the spread of it, for spreading it across the globe will eventually get us There. We are also encouraged to become disciples, to buy and read many more books and attend many seminars on it, and how to practice and perfect it for ourselves. This self-imagined guru, like many, has endless problems with This Here Now and plenty of steps we can take to escape it.

The primary need is for Them, over There, and That situation in which They live, to change. This teacher's call to personal spiritual peace seemingly can not be realized until every one of Them is fixed up and living in some vague sort of spiritually aligned fashion. It's up to us to change It, and Them; to help the guru and his disciples fight their particular good fight. Or something.

But, Gregory...

Alice pointed out...

> *...new things begin to immediately get old. Your culture does not need anything new. You need something Now – something perpetually fresh and focused on the truth that This Here Now is the original Dream coming true. You need simply Look Again.*
>
> *It's like this, Gregory. It's as though you were sitting around chatting with God, and God asked how things might go in your idea of Heaven. Of course you had quite a few ideas about how Others would act, and how they might be fed and clothed, and what they would and would not say and do, and so on. You were ready for this one, as most humans think they are.*
>
> *But as you began to speak God smiled and said No. Please show Me.*
>
> *And Now, Gregory, you find yourself Here, waking up with your Fellow Beings, waking up with me.*

And so I have come to see that indeed This Here Now – the Human Opportunity – *is also* the spiritual Opportunity, the Spiritual Experience.

And the Spiritual Experience is of course the Experience of Unity – an Experience of Unification with the Original Unity that our culture has taught us that we have been separated from

— the underlying Unity of the Universe, of Being, as we know it.

And every current popular tradition, including the scientific ones, has a story of creation that begins with One Thing — a.k.a. Unity. And these stories proceed, each in their own fashion, through Time to a state of Unity once again. Unity Unified, so to speak.

And the funny thing Alice pointed out is this:

If it begins with Unity, and it ends with Unity, then what else could this possibly Be but Unity? What else could This Here Now be but the Opportunity to Express and Experience Unity, Gregory?

This Is It.

This Here Now:
One Opportunity for Unity
Beyond immunity.
But you start with me: Feign indignity
As though I can't see
You label Others, Many, Duality.
Though Unity is what you claim to Be
What you want to see
It's what you speak to Other
Holler at Another
The essence of your Dream
The peace of which you scream
The peace that pass beyond
all knowing This is One.
This is It. Joy & Fun.
The Good Thing: Already come
Here Becoming on and on
Here It Now Be. Eternally.
So Be One With Me.
Joyfully
Express and Receive.
Sing Unity.
Be.
One Here Now.

…an Alice poem

A Now Exspirientuality Story from Alice

Once upon a LifeTime shared lived EverySelf, SomeSelf, NoSelf, and AnySelf.

When EverySelf was busy doing the Important Thing (IT), SomeSelf was sure that NoSelf was doing IT.

NoSelf *was* doing IT, convinced that "AnySelf can do IT if I can. I am NoSelf. I admit I am doing IT, but I am hardly *doing* IT. SomeSelf does IT far better, and I am NoSelf compared to EverySelf. Won't things be grand when EverySelf does IT!"

NoSelf kept an Image of SomeSelf that AnySelf was sure to Aspire to, for SomeSelf, according to legend, had done it like NoSelf would again. Books had been written and handed down through Time. "EverySelf wants to be like SomeSelf," said NoSelf. "If they're AnySelf, that is."

"One day I will be like SomeSelf, doing IT as well as AnySelf. When EverySelf does the Important Thing like SomeSelf once did, life will be heavenly."

And so it never-ends: EverySelf *is* doing the Important Thing, arguing that IT is not getting done because NoSelf is doing what SomeSelf has done better than AnySelf ever will again.

Perspective on a Now Point of View

I've taken the opportunity to write this book in order to share some things that Alice has shared with me over the years—some things regarding Opportunity, Humanity, and mostly Unity. It often feels a bit silly, but the silliness is actually something I am coming to enjoy. I think the silliness pervades because it would seem that so much of what we have to share is obvious. Jesus is said to have remarked something along the lines of, "The kingdom of Heaven is spread upon the Earth, but men do not see it." Many have said simply, "This is It!"

Unity is Here Now, right in front of us, for sure, but somehow humans don't see it. I most certainly was looking the Other way for the better part of a half-century. Our cultures tend to make Unity a very basic fact of our most basic cultural stories, and then label it "not-Unity." We call it duality, multiplicity, the many. These stories begin with The One and proceed to label it divided at every turn.

Thus we do not honor Unity because we do not see it. We do not think we see it, we do not speak as though we see it, and we do not act as though we see it. We do not think it is Here Now, we do not speak as though it is Here Now, nor do we act as though Unity is Here Now. We really don't *believe in* Unity, and thus we cannot *be livin'* Unity. We neither see it nor are inclined to exercise anything more than intermittent faith that This Here Now could possibly be Unity. While it is said quite often that "We are all One," few understand that it is more than a figure of speech, and fewer believe it or behold it.

Humans do not generally tend to go about our daily lives as though we See One Thing or are immersed in Unity. We do not tend to act as though we are One, which plays itself out through ever-persistent exceptions to Absoulute ideas. Beautiful concepts such as The Golden Rule come to bear highest testament to the idea that rules are made to be broken. So many times when a Golden Opportunity arises, a Golden Exception rules the Now moment.

Of course exceptions to Unified guidelines *must* rule the Now if we do not *See* Unity. Our stories have convinced many of us that This Here Now is *an exception to* Unity. The stories are telling us that whatever we Experience Here Now is like the original exception to Unity! Our stories tell us that Unity is beyond Existence. It's *Other Than* This Here Now.

This presents a glorious Opportunity, for the problem is simply one of Perspective. When we see more than One Thing, we tend to see Other. When we see Other we put forth ideas like The Golden Rule, which is Other-Centric, Other-Reliant. Although it speaks to ideas of Self-Consideration, it does so from a Perspective of Other-Consideration. In a World of Unity, a World of One, there is No Other.

Life is a journey of The Self. It's a journey of Self-Realization, Self-Discovery, Self-Fulfillment, those sorts of things. This is conceptually true in both the personal sense of OneSelf and the grand sense of One Self – a.k.a. Unity.

Thus it is at first critically important to shift from a perspective that sees Self and Other to a perspective that Sees Only The Self. One Thing. One. Unity. It's a simple/profound shift from Divisive Vision to Unifying Vision.

In this way we leave behind the divisive concept of Other and stick with Unifying, Absolute ideas such as Self and Being. In fact, it's important to agree on the idea and use of

Absoulute[4] terms, which are essential for anyone that would like to engage Unity.

Absoulute terms are labels for *Ideas with No Other Side*. Ideas that are all-encompassing, like Unity and Universe. They are Unifying terms. We have begun by recalling that at the very basis of every language and story that explains our Existence is an Absolute idea of Unity – an idea of One Thing with No Other Side, so to speak. Absoulute terms allow us to proceed from this recollection as they remind us that Absoulutes are far more than possible. We are aware of a very important One here and now, for we live both *in* and *from* this Absoulute Unity that is the Universe.

And so Unity is an idea that has No Other Side. The possibility of something besides Unity is beyond consideration, by agreement. Just as our Universe has No Other Side, so too Unity is, well, ummm, Unity. The One. It.

Of course we can *speculate* about what might be Other Than our Universe, and it can be a great deal of fun to do so. It can even bring about real-world benefits via the sciences and philosophies. Even the religions and spiritualities lay claim to advances from speculation about what might be Other Than This Here Now. We can make up wonderful speculations about these "not-Universes" and define them with fantastic sets of rules and laws and ways in which things might behave and so on. We can imagine them to have many, many dimensions – far beyond the three/four we perceive in the Universe.

Likewise we can speculate about things called Duality and Multiplicity, the Ten Thousand Things, Other. We can come up with all sorts of fantastic ways in which Being might go, if there were something outside of Unity. And it seems that we

---

4   One day Alice added the "u" in the midst of the word, and it stuck. I think she did it to remind me of Unity.

even derive real-world benefits from this sort of speculation. But the only possibility for Other-Than-Unity is in our heads. We make it up.

And so we can choose to remember that This Here Now is Unity, for Unity is What Is. And in so doing we can remember to think, speak, and act as though Unity is our Experience. In other words, we can choose to Express Unity, and in so doing we will Experience Unity. It would be like Playing the Unity Game. Just for grins, after eons of not-grins.

The big point is This: The Choosing is the importance of what Alice has come to share. Specifically it is choosing our story to its logical implications. Choosing the obvious. Choosing Unity. There are a bunch of ways to say it, but it is about Choice, plain and simple. Even if it is the choice to *pretend* that we believe our chosen stories of Unity. The point is to choose to demonstrate one's faith in one's story of Unity. Absolute Faith; faith underscored by faith.

There is great talk of Unity from President Obama. He made the point early in his first term that "Instead of driving us apart, our very beliefs can bring us together."[5] We know what he is getting at, but we wish that he would reconsider the use of the word Belief. Our *stories* can bring us together, for our stories are of Unity. They begin with Unity and arrive at Unity, and point to the eternal underlying presence of Unity. With Absoulute Faith in our stories, we need only Look Again.

Belief is misunderstood in our culture. Belief is Attraction[6] stuff: What you Believe In you Be Livin'. Poof! Right Now you Be Livin' – and looking at – what you Believe In. They may not be the beliefs you *think* you hold, or *say* that you hold,

---

5   From an address to the National Prayer Breakfast, February 5, 2009.
6   Perhaps more commonly known as the Law of Attraction.

but you are looking at your deepest beliefs about Life. You Be Livin' them. Here Now. It's instantaneous.

What you see is what you get. Seeing is active, not passive. What you Express is what you Experience. Most humans see the world divided and would express this if asked. Most humans see Self and Other. One and Many. Unity Divided. Hence the Experience of humanity divided, for again, what you see is what you get. As the genie says, "Your wish is my command."

Beliefs only stand the chance of bringing us together if we Choose to Be Livin' what we say we Believe In – our stories of Unity. It's a proactive thing: should we choose to Express it first, we will Experience It. Just as it is with Duality. But many of us wait around for the Experience of Unity before we think we could or should or might ought to try to Express It. Many argue that the current Experience is obviously Duality, because "...look at Them, and That. Over There." Thus, many of us wait around for Perceived Others to act a certain way so we can feel all "One with them," or to live a certain way so we can feel better about OurSelf indirectly through Other.

The point is, Choose to See Unity. Adopt and Proclaim Unifying Vision. There is No Other. This is It!

United We Stand, Divided We Fall. Alice and I wonder if our President actually sees Unity, Here Now. He most certainly is trying to share a Unifying Vision, but we wonder if he actually *sees* Unity like most folks see duality/multiplicity. We certainly hope he does, for our leaders have seen their Fellow Beings divided far too long. Our leaders have long been understood to proclaim Life a struggle of The Many to attain Unity, and have done a fine job of insisting upon and perpetuating the illusion for us. It is a fine Time for a leader that actually sees Unity as he or she moves about the world. Every faith, including scientific, proclaims underlying Unity and suggests fine reasons for seeing it far enough into reality that we can honor it, and feel wonder, awe, response ability and gratitude, for this mystery that is the Gift of a LifeTime.

We do understand though that President Obama likely won't be standing around anytime soon saying, "Look! One Thing! All you see is One Thing! This Here Now is It!" So we'll say it. It needs to be said.

You and we are immersed in The *One* Thing. Unity. The Good Thing is This Here Now. It's all Good.

Time will never get us where we think we Dream of Being, for Time is precisely where we have long Dreamed of Being. Being Here Now in Time is the original Dream coming true!

This is what Alice showed me. It's like the One Choice Story we have to share…

One Choice Thing

When I said this before, somebody called it cliché
But there's one choice thing about love I come to relate
Well all I can do is all I can do, and it's all that I could have done then
If love's the end I desire, isn't it the begin?

There's one choice thing about – peace that I come to suggest
But whenever I do, the fighters are put to the test
The best I can tell you is all I can do. Like in first grade,
simple and clear.
If peace is what I would have, I won't start a war.

There's one choice thing about – changing the world I can say
But whenever I do, blame gets in the way
Well all I can sing is all I can say, and all I can play is my part
If change is the end I would have, maybe it's also the start

There's one choice thing about – god I was charged to remind
But whenever I do, ideas go on trial
Well all I can do is all I can do; god knows I continue to try
If god's the track I am on, is belief the train I should ride?

There's one more thing about – love I come to share
But whenever I do, I wonder what do they hear?
Well all I can sing is all I can say, I'll probably sing it again
If love's the end I desire, doesn't that make it the means?
If love's the end I desire, isn't it the begin?
If love is the end We desire…

The One Exercise: Preface

In order to undertake this Unity adventure properly, there is, appropriately, only One Thing to "do," or "be," or "see," or whatever. The One Thing you "do" is The *One* Thing. The One Thing you "be" is One. The One Thing you see is Unity, Unified.

When I first engaged The One Exercise, what worked for me was the choice to See Only The Self. It elevated everything, immediately.

As we noted earlier there is only Perceived Other in a Universe of One. By virtue of the fact that each of us has the perspective of Being a unique Self, of Being OneSelf, we can say that There is Only The Self. The One Self, we could label it.

This is where it gets interesting...

Life, as noted earlier, is a journey of The Self. And yet, we Exist in the presence of Fellow Beings. This idea of Fellow Beings resolves with the idea of Unity = One Self beautifully, for ideas such as Self-Fulfillment, Self-Discovery, Self-Realization, Self-Help, Self-Consideration, and so forth are realized through every encounter with a Fellow Being! It's the interplay of OneSelf and The One Self, at every turn! The *One* Thing!

In other words, OneSelf engages immediately in Self-Help when One helps FellowSelf – a.k.a. a Fellow Being. One engages Self-Consideration immediately when One is considerate of FellowSelf. One thus lives a LifeTime of intentional, focused Self-Realization, Self-Discovery, Self-Improvement, and so on through One's interactions with countless forms of FellowSelf.

Life has nothing to do with Other-realization. Life's encounters tell us nothing of the problems of Other; Life presents The Self with the Opportunity of Unity – of The One Self Self-Engaged in Self-Realization and Self-Fulfillment with the help of FellowSelf… in the glorious interplay that is Life; the interplay of OneSelf with FellowSelf; the play of the Gods and Goddesses.

Consider the band of angels from the song "Swing Low Sweet Chariot;" This is who FellowSelf truly is. Those with whom we are immersed in this divine play are our band of angels, come Here Now to give a gentle shake and remind us to awaken into our Dream of a Lifetime, to awaken into our Becoming Dreams.

They come to remind us that There only seems like There. *If you get There before I do…*

And we come for FellowSelf, and join their band. *And if I get There before you do…*

The emphasis is on the word "get," as in "to understand" – the idea of understanding that *There* is actually *Here* when we focus just so. *There* is where you are looking and what you are focused upon, even though your feet are beneath you as you walk. From this perspective the object of your focus is every bit as much Here as your feet are; both There and Here are Now. A Unity. You go where you look, which means your There becomes your Here. It's more Now than it seems. Time provides a fortunate buffer, but we come to learn that There is Only Here.

We come to remind FellowSelf that Life is play, ReCreation. Being made in the image and likeness of our Creator, we come to eternally ReCreate – to See our Becoming Dreams Alive. We come to remind FellowSelf that "Row Your Boat" is true.

It's the Being/Becoming thing, as Alice puts it. The original Dream coming true is the Dream of Being, Here Now In Time. Here Now, In Time, we Become. What do we Become? The stuff of Dreams!

∽

<u>*An Absoulute Attitude*</u>

I Am
with Fellow Beings
as I Am
with MySelf.

from Digging the Whole:
The Canine Book of Play

∽

The One Exercise: Meditation on the Streets of Your Life

Alice calls it *The One Exercise*, this Seeing Only the Self thing. Its fun and I highly recommend it for awhile. Well, forever, but start with awhile. If this book found its way into your hands, you may be considering the idea, and This is good. Unity may well be why you came.

If you've ever meditated, or read about people that have, you are likely familiar with a rather peaceful state that is attained. Often it is a state in which some wonderful realizations, or insights, arise. A common lament I have heard, and even lamented prior to The One Exercise, is that this state is difficult to maintain, or attain, in the world beyond the meditation room. I believed it for years, until Alice came along.

The One Exercise is Meditating in RealTime, On the Streets of Your Life, Gregory. The objective in meditation is a simple state of thoughtless awareness. It's the state in which one is fully awake and aware without thinking about anything in particular. It is this peaceful state, often labeled blissful, in which realizations – truly inspired and empowered thoughts – arise. Fresh thoughts, not tired, repetitive thoughts; not thoughts about thoughts about thoughts... These are thoughts that are always right for the moment, often to your surprise. Thoughtless awareness. You know...

The One Exercise provides this RealTime Opportunity immediately. Your meditation room is Now the world at large. Remember that when you go sit in your quiet space it takes a few minutes of clock time in order for you to enter this "timeless" peaceful realm.

Likewise, the One Exercise takes a bit of clock time. Allow your mind time to settle into the new practice, just as you did when you began to meditate, or learn anything new that you wanted to attain proficiency at.

But it truly is easy, for once the novelty of Seeing Only The Self is past, there is precious little to think about. There's nothing to label; it's all The Self! Nothing to ask about; it's The Self. It can be trusted to be ItSelf. One's thinking mind gets bored quickly enough, and can take a much needed rest. It will always be there if it is needed to figure a restaurant tip or help locate the car keys or something. But for the most part the thinking, labeling, judging mind can rest. With nothing to think about you are engaged in instant thoughtless awareness – at the speed of Life!

Initially Alice suggested I label everything an aspect of The Self, mostly to drive the point home to my thinking mind, but also for fun. Thus MySelf began to look out upon HimSelf and HerSelf. GregSelf interacted with LynnSelf and AliceSelf, DogSelf and CatSelf, ClerkSelf and DriverSelf. I found MySelf immersed in a world with TreeSelf and SkySelf, sustained by FoodSelf, transported by CarSelf, and so on. Of course TreeSelf can be seen as CedarSelf and OakSelf, and FoodSelf can be seen as SaladSelf and BrownieSelf and what have you. In the Dream of Unity there are an infinitillion[7] manifestation possibilities.

But after awhile the mind is satisfied and experiences little need to label. The answer repeatedly comes back "It's the Self. Stop asking." And the mind begins to relax, and allow that maybe this One Self thing has it pretty well under control and can be trusted, as it is. It need not be known and kept tabs on in every minute aspect. The seeds of true Self-confidence…

---

[7] Another Alice word.

In addition to being afforded a rest, One's mind is Now also freed up to learn and even Create some new Existence games based on a Unifying Perspective – perhaps some truly genuine ways to help OneSelf and FellowSelf unfold Becoming Dreams. The mind is perfectly capable of living in and from Unity, Here Now. As Alice says, assuming human form – including the wonderful creation that is our mind – enhances our Divinity.

༄

༄

The act of Being,
of assuming physical form
in a LifeTime,
Empowers the Expression
and Experience of One's Divinity.

In no way is It diminished.

One's Divinity is simply
One's direct connection with The One Thing.

One Self realized via OneSelf.

A pair of I's shares a pair of Eyes…

from What Would Dog Do?:
The Canine Messiah's Handbook

༄

The Need to No

Know No Know.
No, it is and isn't so.
Know enough to let it go
When Know is No and
Yes is Know.
Now Go.
Go. Go.
Yo.

        ...an Alice poem

Thoughtless Awareness, The Fruit, and the LifeDreamBoat

This state of thoughtless awareness is referred to as "the peace that passes all understanding" in some traditions. It's a peace that derives from a deeply quiet mind, a mind that is very deeply content. Such a mind no longer "needs to know" everything down to its minutest detail. It has given up grasping at laws and rules to make sense of the One Thing. Such a mind proceeds in faith of the deepest sort, Faith with No Other Side.

Absoulute Faith, Gregory.

"Indeed, Alice."

Going back to the idea that This Here Now might well be the kingdom of Heaven spread upon the earth, we get a glimpse into why this "need to know" is precisely what keeps humanity from seeing Unity, and living a Unified Existence instead of a Dual one. The need to know is analogous to continually eating the apple in the Garden of Eden story.

We should remind the reader that the fruit is from the Tree of the Knowledge of Good and Evil. It's not just the Tree of Knowledge, which is how many humans incompletely recall the phrase. This is important, for Good and Evil represent the larger idea of Duality. It is, in effect, the Tree of the Knowledge of Duality, the Tree of the Knowledge of the Illusion That Unity is Duality.

This should clearly explain why One might not be seeing Unity. Duh! Put down the fruit. It's hallucinogenic.

> *This Need to Know can be seen as a Need to "No!" – to say, and often shout, "No!" at everything One thinks is not "Good." Of course the most basic premise of the not-Good, not-The-Garden argument is Duality, Other, "Look at Them! And That! Over There! This cannot possibly be The Garden." And you grab some more fruit from the Tree to energize for your engagement with perceived and proclaimed Other.*

Eating the fruit brings us into the Realm of the Relative and results in what Alice calls Relative Faith. This is faith underscored by doubt, insecurity, a deep need for ongoing proof of the possibility of Unity. The Fruit of the Tree of the Knowledge of Duality keeps One immersed in the hallucination that This Here Now is Duality, struggling to get back to Unity. There's no Time to live as though this is Unity, for we are busy proving that it is not – proving that Later it will be better, when Duality is Unified.

But the Opportunity of The Garden is precisely the Opportunity to trust that This Here Now is a Gift, the Gift of a LifeTime. Six days of creation, and on the seventh day, rest. We were gifted The Garden and offered a place to chill out and play at the game of – and upon the stage of – Humanity. To be still and enjoy and trust that The Universe will always provide for its own; that The One will always provide for its Ones. Faith or Fruit.

Relative Knowledge can be quite useful, of course, and fun here in our phenomenal existence. The possibility for problems only arises when we get hooked on the hallucination and keep eating the fruit and feeding it to our children, thus regurgitating the Divisive falsehoods of Duality and visiting its sins[8] upon the next generation. The problem arises when we sell the idea that we are Separate and Other.

---

8   *Sin* is used here in the sense of its original meaning, *to miss the point.*

We move into the realm of the aforementioned peace when we move beyond a certain sort of belief in — and our addiction to — the fruit and its Relative hallucinations, and when we move beyond the need to know more and more about them. Again, The One Exercise plops us firmly down in this territory, for in its practice we have given up the traditional need to understand, to label and categorize and judge and react and so on. The mind is going quiet, idling down to Peaceful, idling down to Bliss.

To be sure, there is a sense of understanding that accompanies this state; this peace simply goes *beyond* it. It's not a state of feeling or being stupid; One does not lack understanding. There is the same attendant sense of understanding that accompanies us when we walk or brush our teeth or do any routine thing we do with little or no thought. In this peaceful state, One simply goes beyond the understanding aspects of the mind, just as One leaves the thinking mind at the door when going into the meditation room. Just as many of us place awareness into the body in order to ultimately move to an awareness beyond the body, and beyond an understanding of the body. The awareness and understanding of the body are still Here, in the periphery of a larger awareness.

And so, the thinking mind's job is done, for Now. One is Now afforded the full Opportunity of truly learning to Row, Row, Row One's LifeDreamBoat…

༄

At Dawn, when I wake,
I Awake to find Joy
Floating Her Being gently down the stream of Time.
Becoming every Dream she ever Dreamed.

∞

Becoming, She awakens to Dreams
She never Dreamed she has been Dreaming.

∞

In Time Joy floats her Being into the sunset —
A sunset of Dreams she has yet to Dream of Dreaming.

∞

I lose sight of Joy then, and I wonder.
And when I sleep, I Dream of Joy.

∞

And at Dawn, when I wake,
I Awake to find Joy...

...an Alice poem

Lyrics

Story of Our Lies, the[9]

(he said)

I knew it was time to go I
Knew it'd be so hard to show. There
really is no going anyway

I knew it was time to leave it
Hard as it might be believe it
Don't you have one good damn thing to say?

How can you just sit and stare and
Stroke your chin and twirl your hair you
Act as though I've asked you for the time

But time is what you wouldn't give you
Took it, take the way you live - you
Leave the rest of the whole damn world behind

(she said)

Keep time with time
Keep mind in mind
Where really does time come from anyway?

Its time to leave
And I believe
That you don't have one good damn thing to say

Don't look back
It's time to act
You act as though I've asked you for the time

Time to give
Time to live
You left the rest of the whole damn world behind

It's the story of your lies
A tale you chase of compromise
A lie, you say you give yourself away

It's the story of your lies
You want us all to compromise
But damn you I won't give myself that way

It's a world of take and give, the
Oceans become mighty rivers
Flow back home and start it up again

---

9   This song is included on the soundtrack of the movie *Rebellion of Thought* – "a critical look at the role of faith in a post-modern culture" – a film from Paladin Pictures.

I know it is time to leave it	*Time to leave*
Hard as it might be believe it	*I believe*
You don't have to say one good damn thing	*You don't have to say one good damn thing*

Because I know that there is no leaving	*Time to leave*
Hard as it might be believe it – I	*I believe*
Have you with me now I'll have you then	*Have you with me now I'll have you then*

It's the story of your lies
Afraid of love, alibis
A lie, you say you give yourself away

It's the story of our lies it's
Better without compromise
Let's together give ourselves away…

Human Race

Doin' time in a hotel room, window's open city comes inside
The highway runs right up the side of the high-rise, assaulting my ears and my eyes
The breeze feels good but who knows what's in it, so many fumes so little space
Too many cars goin' way too fast – hey – is that the human race
Don't I wanna be in that human race? Don't I wanna win that human race?

Now I've been workin' real hard all of my life but I never seem to get anywhere
I made a lot of money for people I worked for but somehow that wasn't fair
My family and friends they say that's how it is, you gotta love it in spite of the taste
You probly won't win but get in that fast lane and run that human race
You've got to be in that race. We signed you up, boy, take your place.

Now I've been sittin' near the edge checking out the debris pushed aside by the fast-lane cars
And the things I saw are like things you see on a night looking up at the stars
There's a lot of other worlds, a lot of other ways; it's okay to set your own pace
Slow it on down. Take the long way home. Run your own race.
Aha... I think I'll be alright just tagging along.

Grasshopper

Autumn meadow dreaming, grasshopper comes along
Approaching me for answers summoning a song

She questioned me at daybreak, "Where do you go in dreams?"
I said, "Ask of anything, but not the things you've seen."

She asked of reaching heaven, "Where is that distant land?"
I said, "Ask of anything, but not of where you stand."

"Tell me about truth," her brown eyes took me apart
I said, "Ask of anything, but not what's in your heart."

Words are frozen black and white, truth melts into gray
When you live the question, girl, the answer is today

She asked, "Why do you love me? I know that love can fail."
I said, "Ask of anything, but not the things you feel."

The child asked of angels, magic, dragons, myth
I said, "Ask of anything, but not the place you live."

What it's like is not what it is, I told you that before
Experience: the house love built, words push at the door

Words are frozen black and white, truth melts into gray
When you live the question, girl, the answer is today

Her brown eyes asked for secrets, I said not a word
Then I said, "Ask anything, but not of things you've heard."

She asked of love and I said, "One word would go too far,
Ask me about anything, but not the thing you are."

Autumn meadow dreaming, grasshopper comes along
Approaching me for answers, summoning a song

You ask, "What are we seeking, is love the common goal?"
I say, "Ask of anything, but not The One Thing you know."

Music and Speed

Baby, here I am. Off the road again.
The guitar and all's packed, the man pays me cash and I'm gone
The shows were all good, but I'm tired of the road – coming home – now I'm home...

I slide the van into the drive. Full moon; it's 1:05
I uncover the bike. I reach for the key.
The adrenaline surge displaces my need for sleep. Time to fly.

Shift my way up through the gears.
The wind and the motor mix music into my ears.
I'm into the banks and the bends and the curves and the straights.
It's me and the signs and my knee on fast lines they don't paint. And I fly.

Baby, here I am. Lost in your charms again.
Engaging your curves, your body and words and those eyes
Music and speed and you're what I need to survive. And I fly.

Yugen

Would you pass me over that shaker of life, could I have a little more love please?
Pour my ears full of your sweet voice as the dark serenades from the trees
Inhaling your beauty the smoke in the glimpses of light in the dark hides your eyes
As I wonder aloud questions I cannot phrase, so thorough your silent reply

I don't mind anything you say...

Bask in the glow; you light up the room; time stops... you move through our home
You join me at night you teach my heart flight – selfless I know the unknown
Dip and we soar just to do it once more in renewal rote never the same
I've called myself this and I've called myself that but with you no awareness of name

I don't mind anything you do...
I don't mind anything you say...

Time O.T.

Tell me 'bout - - -, do you ever see - - -? Just - - -? Not - - - of a kind.
Tell me 'bout , do you ever see ? Just ? Not   defined.
I would sleep through the night and I'd crash in the light
though I'd heard about Time Overthrown
How I could be stuck There now, stuck free There now. What
time was it? They said, "Then-Now."

Tell me 'bout - -, do you ever meet - -? Just - -? Not - - of a kind.
Tell me 'bout , do you ever know ? Just ? Not   in your mind.
I would sleep through the night and I'd crash in the light 'til
I dreamed about Time Overthrown
How I could be stuck There now, stuck free There now. What
time was it? I knew: "Then-Now!"

Tell me 'bout One, do you ever be One? Just One?
Not One of a kind?
Tell me 'bout Love, do you ever live Love? Just Love?
With no other side?
Now I light up the night and I light up the light.
I set my watch by Time Overthrown
I am not stuck There now, stuck free There now.
I'm In Time. I Am Then-Now.
I should get a watch tattoo, close to the truth, where the hands only point to Now.
The concepts are cool but they're short of the truth and the truth about then is Now.
I only can be then-now I will be all I will be Then-Now.

One Choice Thing

When I said this before, somebody called it cliché
But there's one choice thing about love I come to relate
Well all I can do is all I can do, and it's all that I could have done then
If love's the end I desire, isn't it the begin?

There's one choice thing about – peace that I come to suggest
But whenever I do, the fighters are put to the test
The best I can tell you is all I can do. Basic. Simple. Clear.
If peace is what I would have, I won't start a war.

There's one choice thing about – changing the world I can say
But whenever I do, blame gets in the way
Well all I can sing is all I can say, and all I can play is my part
If change is the end I would have, maybe it's also the start

There's one choice thing about – god I was charged to remind
But whenever I do, ideas go on trial
Well all I can do is all I can do; god knows I continue to try
If god's the track I am on, is belief the train I should ride?

There's one more thing about – love I come to share
But whenever I do, I wonder what do they hear?
Well all I can sing is all I can say, I'll probably sing it again
If love's the end I desire, doesn't that make it the means?
If love's the end I desire, isn't it the begin?
If love is the end We desire…

ifSOWhat

I had this dream and I got to meet god, I just stood there
I mean, I finally get to meet god, what do I do? I freeze.
Fumbled around in my pocket I had noted one question
I'd been planning to ask, but I'd left it at home with my keys

I stood there and stood there and I tapped and I shifted and stood there
And tried to ad lib some profound thing, perhaps a cliché
Then I thought of this really cool joke but I lost the punch line
Then realized god had probly told it first anyway!

Bemuse and bemoan humanity's lot. Witness the eyes how relentless the clock
If I find a key will it fit the lock? And if so... To what?? And ifSOWhat?

Turns out okay, I forgot my catechism. It turned out that god had exactly nothin' to say
A tranquil breeze pulsing color, music, rhythm... Silence in time underlies all the songs ever played

Aware that I dream; awake in my sleep; unfeeling sightless souls walk what we seek
If we could ask would it be for new feet? And if so... for what?? And ifSOWhat?

Then in my dream I was god you were god we just stood there
I mean we finally can do what we want, what do we do? We freeze.
Let diversity give way to the rhythm of laughter; contrast mingle as trees bind fog binds trees

My outform warms an informing brain – this thinking enigma will always remain
If we could ask would the answer pertain?   And if so, to what?   And ifSOWhat?

Repeat first and second verses

I'm out of my form; out of my mind; way out of place and so out of time
If poets ask will the answer rhyme?   And if so, with what?   And ifSOWhat?
Hey do you know, with what? And ifSOWhat?

Revolving Door

Man don't even start with me, I know we've been here before.
I remember the air and the shadows and the sound of the floor.
And the longer I'm here the more I'm sure – the one way out's a revolving door.
So don't even start with me – I know we've been here before.

Don't ask me to prove it. I doubt that I could build a case.
But the feeling grows with me ever since I entered this place.
I know he came in and they did too; man, she was here and so were you.
So don't even try it 'cause I know we've been here before.

And I can almost recall... But it's like waking up from a dream.
Where I know... 'til you ask... then I don't! It's a maddening theme.
But the thought persists; it's funny I'm sure. The one way out's a revolving door.
And I can almost recall... But it's like waking up from a dream.

Don't even start with me. I know we've been here before.
I remember the air and the shadows and the sound of This floor.
I know he came in and they did too. I know she was here. So were you.
So don't even try it 'cause I know we've been here before.

confucius: on shoes

"Relax is somethin' that you just can't do better," he said, "It's only your tension that keeps you together.
Say it not if you gonna want it back," he said, "Time presses on a one-way track.
Mortal antilogy wearing thin. First we choose sides, then we begin.
Haggard version, prolix facts, with your feet on the hard stuff walk on the cracks"

"Seek: you swap belief for truth," he said, "I like walking without shoes.
They fell apart when I left the path, but they were shoes when I got back
Yea, they fit better when I got back"

So many things you say you wish you'd heard, but blame not an egg not for being a bird
Where you are is the only place that you can stand, when the river's to your knees your feet are on land!

Seek: I swapped belief for truth, so I tried walking without shoes
They fell apart when I left the path, but they were shoes when I got back
Yea, just like new when I got back

"Please don't tell me to relax," he said "It's only my tension that takes up the slack!"
And then he pointed, I showed my back, and he slipped away down a well-worn track

Seek: you swap belief for truth; well maybe try walking without shoes
They may fall apart when you leave the path, but they'll be shoes when you get back
And they might fit better when you get back.

Seek: you swap belief for truth, well I like walking without shoes
Though they fall apart when I leave the path, they'll be shoes when I get back
Yea, just like new when I get back
Now some days they come off of the rack
And I wonder if I'll get a shoe contract...
They're gonna be shoes when you get back

Swing Low, Sweet Chariot

Swing low, sweet chariot, coming for to carry me home
Swing low, sweet chariot, coming for to carry me home
I look over Jordan and what do I see, coming for to carry me home
A band of angels comin' after me, coming for to carry me home

Swing low, sweet chariot, coming for to carry me home
Swing low, sweet chariot, coming for to carry me home
I'm sometimes up and I'm sometimes down, coming for to carry me home
But still I know I'm heaven-bound, coming for to carry me home

Swing low, sweet chariot, coming for to carry me home
Swing low, sweet chariot, coming for to carry me home
If you get there before I do, coming for to carry me home
Tell all my friends that I'm coming too, coming for to carry me home

Swing low, sweet chariot, coming for to carry me home
Swing low, sweet chariot, coming for to carry me home
If I get there before you do, coming for to carry me home
I'll cull a hole and I'll pull you through, coming for to carry me home

Swing low, sweet chariot, coming for to carry me home
Swing low, sweet chariot, coming for to carry me home

༶

*Beginning is Creation;
Creation is and always will be the End;
the End is and always will be the Means.
Enlightenment is found in this simple realization:
the time is always Then-Now.*

༶

*Remember always that ReCreation is the
original ongoing idea; commit yourself to play
that is mutually beneficial and rewarding;
to play only as god and dog plays.*

from What Would Dog Do?:
the Canine Messiah's Handbook

༶

∽

The Shaman are Waking Up

This book may remind You that You are a Shaman.

All the World's a Stage for Your Healing Show.

Where will you Show Up?

∽

Shaman

(n) 1698, "priest of the Ural-Altaic peoples," probably via Ger. *Schamane*, from Rus. *shaman,* from Tungus *shaman*, which is perhaps from Chinese *sha men* "Buddhist monk," from Prakrit *samaya-*, from Skt. *sramana-s* "Buddhist ascetic." Related word *Powwow (n)*[10] 1624, "priest, sorcerer," from a southern New England Algonquian language (probably Narragansett) *powwow* "shaman, medicine man, Indian priest," from a verb meaning "to use divination, to dream," from Proto-Algonquian **pawe:wa* "he dreams, one who dreams."[11]

Show

(v) Causal meaning "let be seen, put in sight, make known" evolved c.1200 for unknown reasons and is unique to Eng. (Ger. *schauen* still means "look at").[12]

༄

---

10 Meaning "magical ceremony among N.Amer. Indians" is recorded from 1663. Sense of "council, conference, meeting" is first recorded 1812. Verb sense of "to confer, discuss" is attested from 1780.
11 From Online Etymology Dictionary; www.etymonline.com
12 Ibid

The Now Exspirientuality and Kluge Children's Rehabilitation Center

On the fourth Friday in September 2007, I ran face-first into the overwhelmingly enlightening realization of The Now Exspirientuality. It had been four weeks to the day since I had been introduced to The One Exercise and chosen to engage it. Kluge Children's Rehabilitation Center had been instrumental on both Fridays.

Community Venue shows, in my mind, are performances. I have the sense that most "real" musicians, and most folks in fact, categorize them otherwise, but I do not. I have never been comfortable with the idea that I am somehow special because I "play for *Them.*" Feeling sorry for *Them* is not why I started playing at a nursing home in 1995. I started playing there because I am a musician and I was asked to begin playing there. It's an audience thing…

So I've always rejected the "special me" idea. Most certainly I am participating in something special, but I have never felt like I was the special thing in the mix. It has always seemed a naïve idea to me. And yet, there *was* this recurring thing…

On the fourth Friday in August 2007, I'd had an "emotional" moment when some parents wheeled their child over to enjoy the music. It was clear that he was enjoying the music, and there I was, unable to continue singing. The thought ran through my head that "these are the moments that I do Song-Sharing for, and here I cannot handle it. How lame."

"Gosh, Alice," I had said when I got back to the van. She waits outside KCRC, van parked in the cool morning shade. "It happened again – the emotional thing. What *is* that?" I explained what had transpired.

This is the result of a basic idea that you have, Gregory – the idea that Others should not have to Be as you think this young man is Being. You continue to hold on to the noble but misguided idea that in a perfect world no Others will have to Be like This.

This idea of Poor Others is born of your choice to See the World Divided, to adopt Divisive Vision that sees Self and Other, Duality, Multiplicity. However, as we have lately been discussing, most all of your cultural stories begin with Unity and claim to be headed back to Unity. This begs the question...

"What could This Here Now possibly be, besides Unity?"

Playing at the game of Duality, the game of Multiplicity. The ten thousand things.

The useful point for you is that the emotion you are experiencing and unable to channel into the performance is emotion you do not understand, that's all. This is safe to say, yes?

"Yes. Most definitely. That's a good way to say it, that I want to be able to channel this energy into the moment, not have it detract from it. And I definitely don't understand it."

You simply need to Look Again, Gregory, through the lens of Unifying Vision.

She went on to explain The One Exercise and I went on to engage it. It was an interesting four weeks, and the fresh Now perspective of The One Exercise grew quickly on me. On the fourth Friday in September, again at KCRC, a similar scenario began to unfold when some parents entered the lobby and heard music. They turned their son's wheelchair and he lit up, and they headed my way. I relaxed further into Unifying Vision and the song I was playing. I allowed my eyesight to blur into the middle distance beyond the young man, allowing him into the soft, open musical space, allowing the aspects of Unified Experience to be as they be, and in a moment our eyes came together and…

In a flash I was beside myself, outside of myself, outside of my presence, something… I was still very much Here, playing my guitar and singing, and quite comfortable in that aspect; and I was simultaneously Here, observing, watching the KCRC scene unfold as though I was watching a play from a box seat above the stage. My cosmic partner and host was a profound presence of which I was highly aware, but not in any formal sense, and I know for certain that it was the young man from the wheelchair. There were Fellow Beings observing with us as well, but I do not know who. I know it was comfortable. I know it was all good.

We watched the musical moment unfolding in a sort of crystal orb, like a fragile, oblong, hollow glass ornament. At one point I had the image of those early glass orb ideas of the Universe. The space all around was filled with countless crystal orbs, each a scene; a sparkling crystal Universe dancing with ItSelf like the snow in a well-shaken globe…

And it became very clear to me that there is nothing wrong with this young man, nothing at all. It became very clear that there is nothing wrong with anyone in a Community Venue audience. I'd known it all along, but never like This. The overwhelming inescapability of pure equality was humbling.

As I eased back into a more familiar association with my physical form I felt electrified, and I'm certain I hovered above the seat of my chair on some sort of force field for the remainder of the performance. I wasn't certain what had just happened, and I looked at the young man in his wheelchair. He wasn't letting on anything, but he was digging the music. His whole body was smiling.

༄

One day Samzan was walking through the market and overheard a conversation between an aspiring musician and an agent.

"Book the best audience for me," said the musician. "I will only perform for the best audience."

"Every audience is the best," replied the agent. "There is no audience Here that is not the best."

Upon hearing this Samzan became enlightened.

༄

The Opportunity of Opportunity

It's like this, Gregory. It's as though you were sitting around chatting with God, and God asked how things might go in your Vision of Heaven. Of course you had quite a few ideas about how Others would act, and how they might be fed and clothed, and what they would and would not say and do, and so on. You were ready for this one, as most humans think they are.

But as you began to speak, God smiled and raised a hand to gently silence you, and said, "No, Show Me."

And Now, Gregory, you find yourself Here, waking up with your Fellow Beings, waking up with me.

❦

    The perpetually enlightening realization of The Now Exspirientuality has been and continues to be Opportunity. It is primarily the realization that Life ItSelf is Opportunity; Life is the Opportunity of Opportunity, so to speak. The burden of perceived problems is gone, thus the sense of having been enlightened, having had a burden lifted.
    This realization is based in the ultimate discovery of Unity and Equality – the realization that there is nothing wrong with anyone or anything Here. Those Fellow Beings I formerly perceived as Other than I, and thus as the source of Life's problems, challenges, and obligations, are actually Opportunity. They are the Opportunity for me to stage my show. They are here for me, as I am for them.
    The primary Opportunity my Fellow Beings afford me is the Opportunity of Humanity, for we are all here dreaming a

Dream of, and for, Humanity. We are all here on the stage of Humanity, the stage of Being, putting on our show. We are all here dreaming a Dream of Being Human.

And the Opportunity of Humanity is the Opportunity of *Just As I Am*, for the Dream of Humanity is a Dream of *Just As I Am;* a Dream of being allowed and accepted, *Just As I Am;* of expression and experience, *Just As I Am;* of loving OneSelf, *Just As I Am.*

And this is where the importance of the showman/shaman connection comes in, for the Opportunity of Humanity is a healing Opportunity. We came to heal.

The world is all a stage, and thus each of us is a showman, staging the show of our LifeTime, our show of *how it might go*. And a showman, as Alice points out, is a shaman, a dreamer of healing dreams, one who sees beyond and brings healing visions back to share, to act out with healing intent.

American showmen/shaman, however, have not escaped the hypnotizing effects of physical currencies in our society. Early showmen traveled in medicine shows, largely selling products that they (knowingly) falsely claimed would heal. Our intoxication by and resulting focus upon cash currencies is arguably at the basis of this shift, for cash currencies are of perceived value, just like false medicines.

Shaman deal in the exchange of Soul Currency, which is an offshoot of their deep recognition of both human value and individual value – the value of Being, and of individuals Being.

Awakening shaman are aware that we live for the exchange of Soul Currency. They know it is an Absolute Gift, that Soul Currency is inexhaustible and tends to flow more freely to those who give it freely. They know how to exchange Soul Currency for whatever they need in the moment, for they understand it to be the basis of all physical currencies.

༄

It's the song that burns
It's the wheel that turns
It's the way we sing that makes 'em dream...

...from Live's *Selling the Drama*[2]

☙

The showman/shaman recognizes also the Opportunity of Response Ability. Being brings with it the joyous ability to respond in whatever fashion we choose. This ties in closely with the idea that Here is only Opportunity. No problems, no responsibilities in the obligation sense. The Opportunity to respond, to express *Just As I Am,* to respond with our show of *how it might go.*

We share this Absolute Gift of Response Ability with our Fellow Beings. Our Fellow Beings do not present us with burden or obligation; they present us with the Opportunity to ReCreate our world in this moment by responding from our idea of *how it might go.* When we respond from the shaman's recognition of equality, and human and individual value, the world is recreated Now, Here.

*Is This Here Now what my Gift of Time is for?
That's the perpetually relevant question, Gregory.*

Early Life can gift you all the talent for the haul;
Its gracious arms will lift you and its gravity will let you fall...

...from Tom Proutt's *Apply the Brake*[3]

༜

And, oh my... the showman/shaman revels in the Opportunity of "Row Your Boat." This is no less than the Opportunity of Professional Youth, the Opportunity to bring your art and creativity to the forefront of your Life. Professional Youth displaces a mid-Life, or later-Life, need to become again as children.[13] Every one of us rows a perfectly equipped LifeDreamBoat to the shores of this existence. It is equipped with every imaginable Absolute Gift we'll need to unfold our highest dreams of humanity, to stage our play. Children have a sense of play about the conduct of Life and the most fitting response to what is. This childlike wonder, sense of play, and fearless exploration and sharing of one's world and one's Absolute Gifts can carry into adult Life, even as childish tendencies are left behind.

"Row Your Boat" also speaks to the Opportunity of Time Overthrown, of shifting to a more complete understanding of Time as the basis of a LifeTime. Our seat in the boat is like the Now, the still point of time in which we always experience our Life. It's always Now, no matter what our watch may say, or if it is light or dark outside. The ancient Greeks called this aspect of time *kairos*. The stream upon which we row our boat is like

---

13 I often wonder about the link between this idea and situations wherein older folks revert back to childish tendencies – as though some of the conditions we see in seniors arise because Life was always such a serious matter; they did not play at Life for decades. It's like nature always gets its way or something.

clock time, or *chronos*. Chronos is the only aspect of time that most of us are familiar with, a rapid stream that flows from a perceived past most quickly thru the present and into an imagined/unimaginable future.[14]

> *It's the Opportunity to recognize that This Here Now is precisely what your Time is for, Gregory.*

And so "Row Your Boat" also speaks to the Opportunity of the ReCreator – the creator made in the image of The Creator. This is mythology of course, which presents the immediate Opportunity to NOT get hung up on images of what "The Creator" might look or be like. The point is to Create – to *play at* Creation, hence ReCreation, a.k.a. recreation...

We are quite obviously surrounded by This from which we came. Move on. Back to your show. If your show is a show of being hung up, demanding more and more proof that Life is your Opportunity for the Good Thing, well then carry on. But if you'd like to move along into creation free of this burden, feel free to engage The One Exercise and shift into the Opportunity of the showman/shaman, and Professional Youth.

Having chosen to move into a more Now sort of show, I am giving ever-fresh meaning to the Opportunity of *Think Global, Act Local*. It's clear to me that every human interaction in every moment Here Now is the Opportunity to heal my entire world. It's all fine and good to bring my music to a benefit for the hungry in Darfur, but it's infinitely more effective to share with the hungry in my community; this applies to those hungry both for food and simple acts of humanity; simple acts of art, and kindness... This is where the Absoulute Gifts come in, for

---

14   For many it moves from a perceived undesirable past, through a barely tolerable present, towards a hopefully better future, although there is much doubt underlying their faith in this future.

they are gifts that are best given. They replenish themselves in multiples. They are of infinite supply.

So we're shaman, and we've come to stage a healing show. There's one more thing though – well, One Thing...

Turns out that this healing thing is actually a Self-healing thing; turns out we come to Self-heal, not heal Others.[15] Self-healing is all-encompassing, which is the funny sort of paradox I have finally come to understand. I am comfortable enough with the idea that the music I bring into Community Venues is medically healing in a manner that has been scientifically documented. What we really might ought to document, though, is the degree of showman-healing that takes place – the degree to which the performer is healed – for music is not a one-sided game. If I perform my healing show in a forest...

The One Exercise is the only way to Self-heal, for there is only The Self. And a series of steps to get there are silly, for there is only one step I can take: This step, the Now step.

Besides, There is only Here... Consider the last verse of "Swing Low, Sweet Chariot," which begins with the line "If I get there before you do." As we've said, the phrase "get there" is not about traveling, it's about understanding, perception.

Courtesy of Alice, The One Exercise, and our friends in Community Venues, I *get* There. There is Here. That is This. Other is Self. The apparent two are a perceptible Unity. The

---

15   This rather reveals the weakness of spiritual books aimed at fixing up the world, and self-help/self-improvement books aimed at fixing up the people in it: they shift immediately to an Other-focus. The reader's world becomes a series of problems, challenges, and obligations defined by the situations of perceived Others. There are Poor Others that we do not wish to be like, and feel that no one should have to be like. And there are Fortunate Others that we desire to be like. Today's self-improvement is defined and gauged by the situation of Others and how we see ourselves relative to them. Our idea of how it might go in Heaven relies heavily upon the absence of certain Others and the presence of Other Others. Alice says the self-help section in bookstores might be more aptly named Other-help.

separation is a function of our creation, a function of our perception of Time and Space, the distance in our eyes...

I posted something on a spiritual forum once, saying that this enlightening experience of The Now Exspirientuality is like waking up at the crack of dawn when I was at the beach as a child. There would be three or four families in the same house, and five or six kids sleeping in the same room. I posted the fact that when I'd wake up early I would tiptoe out in bare feet and slip quietly down to the porch to enjoy the quiet sunrise. I'd let my fellow shaman snooze as long as they'd like; I felt no need to holler, "Hey, yo! I'm awake. Come on, you sleepy lazy fools, you're screwing it all up!!"

My comment was well received, and one fellow posted a wonderful follow-up question. He said, "But Greg, what if you are off to see Disneyland? What if you are off to see the pyramids? This is what you are awakening into; should you not bring your fellow beings along? Should you not awaken them?"

My reply was simple, and short.

"What I am awakening to is the fact that these divine fellow beings are precisely the pharaohs and the queens, the princes and the princesses. They are Minnie and Mickey, Donald and Daisy, Goofy and Pluto. They are the creators, the builders of pyramids and magic kingdoms.

"They are awakening just fine, in their own time. It is an honor to wake, and walk, among them. It is a grand honor to be Here as they awaken to their true Self and begin to consciously bring their magic to Life. And it is the grandest honor to find myself in This presence as I awaken to my own magic."

Alice has been showing me how shaman can collapse time and space by virtue of perspective, which she breaks down further as intent and focus in this case. It's like where we are headed and where we look when we walk, or roadrace a motorcycle. Those who look down at their feet or front tire tend to utilize more time and space to arrive[16] than those who look well ahead, focused on the destination. Those who tend to be distracted by where they don't want to go tend to end up precisely there, and those who focus on perceived Others lose sight of their own intent.

She's showing me lots of Now things available to the awakening showman/shaman. But that's an unfolding story, a becoming song...

---

16   That is, if they arrive at all. We don't recommend roadracing while looking at your front tire, or walking while looking at your feet for that matter.

∽

I look over Jordan and what do I see?
Comin' for to carry me home...
A band of angels all around me
Comin' for to carry me home...

Recommended Reading/Listening

Zen and the Art of Motorcycle Maintenance, by Robert M. Pirsig

The Way of Life: Lao Tzu; the Classic Translation by R.B. Blakney

Anything written or recorded by Alan Watts, particularly *The Book: On the Taboo Against Knowing Who You Are*

Anything written by Joseph Campbell, particularly *The Inner Reaches of Outer Space*

The Power of Myth video series featuring Joseph Campbell with host Bill Moyers

Mr. God, This is Anna, by Fynn

Zen Flesh, Zen Bones, by Paul Reps and Nyogen Senzaki

The Power of Now, A New Earth, Stillness Speaks, and *Even the Sun Will Die,* by Eckhart Tolle.

Illusions, and *The Bridge Across Forever,* by Richard Bach

The *Conversations with God* books, by Neale Donald Walsch

Any R.E.M. CD, especially *Fables of the Reconstruction, Life's Rich Pageant,* and *Reveal.* No, really anything by R.E.M. Go online and get the lyrics...

Farm Jazz, a CD from Tom Proutt

Pancake Mamma, a CD from Tom & Emily

Sleeping Giants, a CD from Thomas Gunn

Talking to the Dead, a CD from The Rusticators

Image Credits

Alice on Box photo by Lynne Brubaker. www.brubakerphoto.com

CD Cover, Alice/Time Overthrown oval, Alice standing in archway, both shots of Alice with the metronome, and the photo of Greg holding Alice by Browning Porter. www.browningporter.com

Messiah Is In, Guru Gas, Van tailgate, and Alice snoozin' in crate photos/illustrations by Greg Allen Morgoglione.

Artwork, cover photos and majority of the booklet photos for the CD *It's Time That Time Was Overthrown* were by Browning Porter. Photos taken at Lambeth Colonnades, University of Virginia.

Additional Websites

Alice & Greg	www.TheNowExspirientuality.net
	www.GregAllenMusic.net
	www.GraspingAtLaws.net
	www.timeoverthrown.blogspot.com
Thomas Gunn	www.ThomasGunnMusic.com
Tom Proutt and Emily Gary	www.Tom-and-Emily.com

Julie Caran	www.myspace.com/bluestonesky

Abbey Linfert and	www.TheRusticators.com
Chris Amsler

Jeff Romano	www.GreenwoodStudio.com

EndNotes

[1] © 1986 Night Garden Music, Administered by Warner-Tamerlane Music Publishing; lyric changed with permission.

[2] Selling The Drama
Words and Music by Edward Kowalczyk, Chad Taylor, Patrick Dahlheimer and Chad Gracey
Copyright © 1994 by Universal Music – Careers
International Copyright Secured   All Rights Reserved

[3] ©2003 Tom Proutt / Rock 'n Fish Records / Flatt 'n Squirrel Music
All Rights Reserved.

Made in the USA
Charleston, SC
12 January 2010